A Woman's Journey

Cindy Ross

Copyright 1982 by Cindy Ross
First Printing by East Woods Press, 1982
First Printing by Globe Pequot Press, 1988
Fifth Printing by Appalachian Trail Conference, 1990

Library of Congress Cataloging in Publication Data
    Ross, Cindy
        A Woman's Journey on the Appalachian Trail
            1. Backpacking -- Appalachian Trail 2. Appalachian
        Trail -- Description and Travel I. Title
        GV199.42.A6 BR67   917.4   81-17343
        ISBN 0-917953-42-8

Printed in the United States of America

The Appalachian Trail...
over 2,000 miles and through 14
States, it traverses the mountaintop ridges from Georgia to Maine.

Chapters

To Jim Brett...
who first believed

In Philadelphia, in a high-rise... I exist. Have done so for two years... attending art school, striving to fulfill some dream of becoming a painter.

Lately I'm slipping... out of touch... losing the meaning of life. I look down eighteen stories to diseased oaks, diseased pigeons, confused humans running the maze. My God, I don't belong here — I'm wasting my life.

Inspiration... I can't find it here. It has to come on differently. Enough of street scenes, still lifes, exercising on Rittenhouse Square.

There's been this urge... this drive, coming from a certain dream. A dream to do the Appalachian Trail from Springer Mtn. to Katahdin. It burns in my heart more and more these days - kills my brain with challenge - occupies my day-dream thoughts.

Thoughts of crisp air, crystal wild water, uncomplicated flow of days - REBIRTH! I need to get on with my life. I am going to do it. Now! In body and spirit I will commit myself. I'm on my way.....

1 The Early Days

A mountain is the noblest piece of nature. They have the most strength. The most grandeur. The most power. They reach up. They attain great heights and on their summits they share these incredible feelings with you.

Testing our bodies is important and seemingly necessary these first weeks and the Georgian Mountains are becoming our training ground. We push and push until either something breaks or our spirits fray. No one makes us push so hard
...we just do.

Mountains are everywhere down south. They don't run in a long ridge as they do further north. The land is just covered with them. Sometimes we have to go over 6-7 a day. This does a real job on our bodies... rips the achilles tendon right away from the bone and utterly destroys the knees. Every town stop, a few more hikers drag their battered bodies and spirits onto Greyhounds heading home.

8

We travel in a small family these early days, sharing everything from back-rubs to extra clothing to our hopes and fears.

Hikers come from all over the country... bankers, chefs, attornies, graduate students, even courageous men with families back at home and single women alone. Some running away. Others running towards. Escapists, searchers, the carefree and the intense. From all different backgrounds, from all different life-styles and all are equal... Women are scarce, but we certainly aren't catered to. All do their share. There is weakness and there is strength, but it is intermingled. Even that is shared.

9

Not many hikers have partners, but it is the most rewarding way to hike! I am blessed with the good fortune of having one... Colleen Rearden, my childhood friend. Together we dreamt of log cabins and being mountain women and hiking the Appalachian Trail.

She gives me strength when I am broken. She mends my frayed spirit when I feel defeated.

Every month, without fail, I become very sick with menstrual pain. Cramping and crying and doubling over with pain. We always seem to have a horrendous climb on these memorable days... the first mountain is Blood Mountain... as absurd as it sounds.

Colleen coaches me through these days... trying to bolster my spirit and make me laugh.

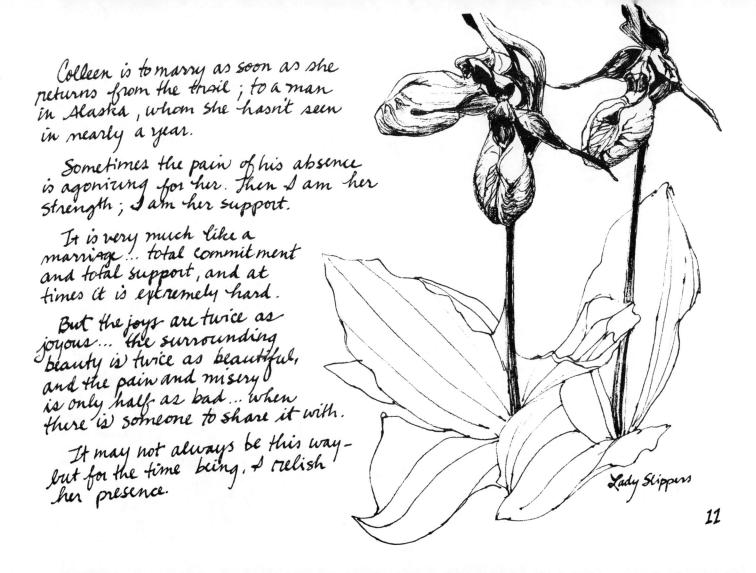

Colleen is to marry as soon as she returns from the trail; to a man in Alaska, whom she hasn't seen in nearly a year.

Sometimes the pain of his absence is agonizing for her. Then I am her strength; I am her support.

It is very much like a marriage... total commitment and total support, and at times it is extremely hard.

But the joys are twice as joyous... the surrounding beauty is twice as beautiful, and the pain and misery is only half as bad... when there is someone to share it with.

It may not always be this way— but for the time being, I relish her presence.

Lady Slippers

11

It can get terribly cold in these Smoky Mtns. damp, wet, bone chilling rains.

One time, my body is so numb and cold from the rain, that I begin loosing all motor control...

Fontana Dam

APPALACHIAN TRAIL
- Shuckstack Lookout 3½
- Birch Spring Gap Shelter 5
- New Found Gap 37½
- Davenport Gap 68½

CAMPING PERMITTED ONLY AT DESIGNATED CAMPSITES
CAMPING PERMITS REQUI

I start tripping, my hiking stick continually falls out of my hand. I can't use my muscles and I start to cry. Fear is lurking in the shadows — fear of hypothermia. It is time to quit. Time to crawl into the sleeping bag and die.

That night my partner takes care of me. She cooks the supper, does the dishes, hangs the food.

12

This giving and taking is very important out here on the trail. The stronger one always helps the one that is weaker at the time.

And when you are BOTH weak, the one that can conjure up the most amount of strength just knows that it's all up to her

... And then there are times when we are so hot that when we cross creeks we just submerge our entire heads into the water, open wide And drink like a horse.

... Sometimes it takes all of our self-control to refrain from wallowing bodily in the refreshing liquid. But there are more times when we happily give in.

As I hike north, my personal relationship with the mountains is becoming almost sacred. I am going up. Up to meet my Creator. Up to where the sweet wind can caress my tired body like a Father's loving hand.

On these mountaintops I am born again. Every pore is filled with life-sustaining energy. Up here I find the strength to go on.

To be this intimate with the mountains, I know I must live there for a time. Learn all her colors... experience all her moods ... be in her storms as well as her suns.

Charlie's Bunion

"Tennessee Walker" is an 18-year-old backwoods boy out to conquer the whole Appalachian Trail. His real name is Doug Walker and he hails from Tennessee, so his new name only seems appropriate.

He has the typical book-learning of most kids his age, but he has the firsthand outdoor experiences of a 40-year-old mountain man.

Rattlers and copperheads are no match for him. He'll kill them and clean them. Roast them over a fire and tantalize the hiker's taste buds. Then he'll dry out the skins and make belts and bands for his hat.

Brook trout are caught with his bare hands, or by using a good-sized rock. Eight grouse were brought to their deaths by his hiking stick as they zoomed by him on the trail. All were disposed of very ecologically... in his stomach.

He is as "at home" in the forest as the virgin hemlocks and it is refreshing to see somebody so genuinely unique and untouched by society's rules of behavior.

"Traveler" follows no rules of behavior either.

He is as unique and individual a dog as you can find. He was picked up by my friend, Bob Kelleher, in Hot Springs, N.C. A stray... but nonetheless, ripe and ready to start on a new adventure, or so his daddy thought.

The dog follows everybody, but is never with his owner. Bob is always far behind, weighed down by the moist, tender, and terribly heavy GAINESBURGERS! Traveler will eat nothing less.

He is no dummy He knows when he has a good thing going. Sometimes he isn't in the mood to hike... no bother, he'll lay down on the trail... Bob will come along and carry him!

16

At one time or another, Alberto Foscani has been a waiter in nearly every classy restaurant in nearly every major city all over the world.

One day he decided he needed a change... never having backpacked before he set out to conquer the entire length of the Appalachian Trail.

This terribly amusing character, who talks like he stepped right off the boat, adds so much color to our daily lives.

He goes ranting and raving, with true Italian temper, through these southern mountains... swearing in Italian and wondering where in the hell that shelter is.

But his generosity and compassion so typical of his people, finds him a place in many of our hearts.

27

We now come to a class of people all their own...
"THE WEEK-ENDER." We learned very early in our walk not
to stay at shelters planted by a road. They are constant
meccas for local teen-agers to party! Graffeti nearly always
covers the walls - beer cans and broken glass grow out of
the ground like weeds. Sometimes parts of the shelter will
be disassembled for
use as firewood
or whole living
trees cut down
for this purpose.
Sometimes we
are awakened
by carloads of
kids coming -
slamming doors,
breaking bottles,
bellowing curse
words through-
out the woods.
This is wilderness?

18

These episodes don't happen often, but it only takes one time to realize why the Appalachian Trail Conference is so set on relocating all of the shelters away from the roads.

Most of the people hiking out on the week-ends though are the most pleasant, the most helpful, the most genuinely happy to be here and share the beauty with us.

One such person is Budd Webb. He is a teacher and a craftsman and wears a beautiful hand carved cedar belt buckle with A on it, that he made himself.

He isn't in the shelter five seconds before I begin marveling at its beauty. Then he quickly takes off his buckle and presents it to me as a gift. It doesn't matter to him that he is only beginning his trip and has to walk the rest of the way with his pants falling down.

20

Town stops are looked forward to; as is the sun's warmth after many, many days of rain. No matter how much you are in love with the woods — EVERYTHING gets old after awhile. You long for a little diversion in your hiking life, and towns are the answer.

The towns that shine above the rest are the ones that have hostels in them — true oases in the wilderness. They can be anything from big old farmhouses to hand built barns to the basement of a church to a firehouse. They are usually owned and operated by a local church and the only charge is a small donation.

They are centers
where hikers can come
together - to shower,
to sleep, to enjoy some
of the comforts of home
as we continue on
our journey.

These rejuvenation centers are
for our use, our sharing, our comfort.
A result of someone else's caring.
Someone that we don't even know!
Someone who just understands hikers
and possesses that precious gift
of giving.

Sometimes we find a local bar that sports live bluegrass music. We kick back and get _real_ loose.

Alcohol and long distance hikers don't mix. Our bodies absorb it like a sponge and in no time at all, we're doing things that we've never done before.

Like dance. And do we dance. Gym-shorted legs flying, vibram soles stomping. People do-si-doing and swinging their partners all over the dance floor.

Even the laundromat in Damascus, Virginia was no exception. There is an ancient juke box there, with five plays for a quarter on it. All of the top 40... from 10 years ago!

On tops of the washing machines we dance, up and down the aisles. The local wash women just shake their heads and say

"Those crazy hikers."

23

Food is always on our minds. We seem to be constantly hungry. As soon as one meal is finished we begin planning what to have at the next. One hiker consumes a half-gallon of ice cream and a 9" pie upon entering town, trying to fill the void.

The hottest item on a hiker's trail menu is that infamous GORP. Its base consists of 1/3 peanuts, 1/3 raisins, and 1/3 M+M's. All kinds of assorted goodies can be added to enhance its taste... dried fruit, shredded coconut, sunflower seeds, even peanut butter morsels if available.

Many hikers consume their entire stock of gorp from a new food drop* before they even look at their other food; eating the little treasures for every single meal and snack until it is completely depleted.

* food drop... boxes of supplies mailed to Post Offices along the trail.

My last town stop with my partner is just outside Whitetop, Virginia. Jimmy Hayes lives there, an old friend from my iron ore mining days who happens to own land right by the trail here in southern Virginia; and back home in Pennsylvania!

This multi-talented man is also a professional fiddle player and he promises that we wouldn't leave until we experience some real mountain music.

He takes us on a jeep safari ride all day long - roaming the mountains and visiting backwoods grocery stores where the men actually drive their tractors to shop instead of cars.

Inside, they all sit around the pot-bellied stove in the middle of the store, on sofas and chairs that look like they come right out of a Hope Rescue Mission Catalog.

They all play banjo and fiddle and sing their little mountain hearts out... no teeth in their mouths.

Jimmy is going back to Pennsylvania for a few days and he tempts us with this offer...

25

"How would you like to visit your folks and in 2 days I'll bring you right back to where you left off?"

How can we resist. I picture in my mind, jumping onto my parents bed at 6 in the morning... they'll sit up in their sleepy stupor with a look of total disbelief on their faces and think they are seeing a vision ... we have to go!

When we return our trail family has moved ahead. Colleen feels lost. We kill ourselves and try to catch them for a few days. We spend the nights wide awake flexing our legs and rubbing our feet because we are in such agony. The soles of our feet feel like ground hamburger from doing such big days.

To me, it isn't worth it. What about living for today? Why not enjoy the time and space we are in, regardless of who is present or absent?

She chooses to go on. 20+ mile days is not my idea of fun, so I stay behind. She says "I'll see you up the trail." I know we'll never hike together again.

There at Wapiti Shelter by the Dismal Creek, we part. Very appropriate I am about to embark on a journey of extreme loneliness and despair... ALONE.

Me and Grandmom

2 Alone

Loneliness.

That's a solo hiker's main enemy; even more so than the most extremes in weather.

I enjoy my own company; can entertain myself. I'm not one of those problem people that psychology books talk about - people who dislike themselves and have to learn to be their own best friend.

I am fairly stable and secure. I don't think hiking alone will affect me all that much.

Besides,
look at all I can learn.

A watch doesn't seem to fit into my lifestyle. I like the easy flow of things... resting when tired, eating when hungry, rising with the sun's first long rays and sleeping when its dark. Its that simple and uncomplicated on the Appalachian Trail.

You learn to feel the time of day too. You watch the sun's path in the sky, the rising and setting of the moon. You feel the breezes picking up and dying off; the animals stirring about and quieting down.

Even fore telling the weather becomes second nature. You notice wind direction, cloud formation. You can actually FEEL rain approaching. The air becomes dead heavy, thick, like oatmeal. Here breathing becomes a chore. There's no breeze to cool you off and the sweat rolls off your body like a dripping wet dish rag.

Bugs light. Animals disappear and there's a certain foreboding in the air. Then the wind picks up. It blows fiercely and turns all the leaves upside down so their light under sides are showing. I always hike fast at this time... hurrying along trying to outwalk the storm. Perhaps its the energy all around me. Perhaps it's an element of dread.

Despite inclement weather, I still enjoy sleeping under a tarp. Tents are like houses to me... tight-secure enclosures hiding me from the world of night and blocking that incredible breeze that constantly brushes across my face.

I'm lying here observing all the forest creatures: Chipmunks scurry closer when I'm alone and quiet. I can observe a deer's habits for hours if I sit motionless and keep silent; even watch a millipede lazily weave himself in and out of twigs by my side.

I notice these pieces of life when there's no one to talk to. I begin to feel like a wild animal— unhuman, especially when I don't see other humanoids for days on end.

It's our nature though, to look and long for others of our own kind to share and communicate with.

Like the animals, we need our own around us.

Brown
Thrasher

I don't concern myself with wants. I turn my energy into NEEDS. I seem to be quite happy and satisfied when my basic human needs are fulfilled.

Back home I can get caught up in acquiring "things"— unnecessary trivia that clutters up my life and my mind.

Out here, I just want to quench my thirst, crawl under a rock in a storm and have the sun come out to dry me off.

Everything besides this is a special blessing from God... a cool breeze on a mountaintop, a brilliant blue sky, a deep pool to swim in on a hot day. Nothing... is taken for granted.

One learns to make-do.
One learns to make the best of very little.

I use sticks to hold my bun together, large smooth leaves for toilet paper, baking soda for deodorant and tooth paste; and glowing candlelight in place of electricity.

I actually SEW my underwear... mend the elastic, patch my pants, darn my socks. Nothing is thrown away. Even when my clothes literally fall off me, I recycle it and use it as rags. My washing machine is a stream and my dryer is the sun, as my clothes hang on the back of my pack.

I can learn to make-do and do without nearly everything, except people. People who care and love me. People whom I can hug.

We have a very technologically advanced system of communications on the trail. There is a network of registers along the trail; tablets and notebooks for hikers to sign in. News travels from one state to the next in a matter of days. Faster hikers passing by take news ahead up north; south bounders take it to those behind.

We can follow someone's entries for months - knowing their handwriting, their adventures, their souls. When we finally meet up with them, it's like a reunion with an old, old friend.

Through these registers we learn which springs are dry, where stores are, which lakes have leeches and which shelters have porcupines. They even serve as a lost and found. Once an entry read, "Has any body seen my Mom? I lost her on the trail 2 days ago." He had everybody looking for his Mom, people that he's never even met. When they finally were reunited he neglected to sign it in, and many a concerned fellow hiker was still looking for dear Mom several days later.

33

The sun is frying me today. It isn't friendly weather and I'm certainly not traveling in friendly countryside. I come off the mountain into Scorched Earth Gap where the land is so dry and parched that big huge cracks cover the land.

The lower I get into this hell hole, the louder these strange unearthly sounds become. It's a wierd, screaming, buzzing sound. Finally I see one... these strange, insects with big orange eyes. They dive into me, screaming. Cicadas they are, and this is their year in this dreadful valley. Every 17 years they resurrect themselves, crawl out of their holes in the ground, shedding their skins everywhere. They mate, and then they all die, living but a few days in the sunshine.

The noise is so loud that I must stuff gauze from my first-aid kit into my ears to stifle it. I feel like I'm going crazy.

I wonder at the value and purpose of some things in nature. Man's mind cannot comprehend so many mysteries. I suppose that's why we are down here crawling around instead of in celestial heaven controlling the powers of nature.

Flat ridge walking seems like a dream come true. The elevation map reads ⌐‾‾‾‾‾¬... a "cruising trail." But usually there's some catch. This ridge has no water, and boasts hundreds of blown-down trees. There was a terrible ice storm here in Virginia last spring, knocking hundreds of trees down. A good 30 a day I must walk around, doubling the mileage as I travel completely around their branches... stepping over limbs, into limbs. My legs are so scratched and bloody that they look as if they were beaten with whips.

It hasn't rained for days and days and all the springs have dried up. I am so thirsty that I resort to licking the moisture off the leaves of the trees that have fallen across the trail. My mouth is parched. My body is weakened. Never before did I long for water as badly as I do now.

I think back to other hard times that I found myself in. They never seem as bad when you have someone to share them with... lighten the load. I approached such encounters light-heartedly, found amusement in them. Alone it is different. Alone I take life so much more seriously. I know now that life isn't meant to be lived alone.

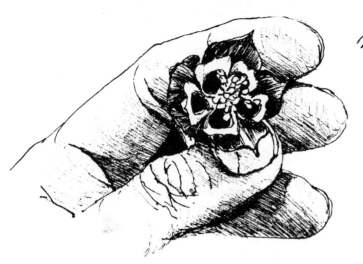

I didn't always feel this way. When I was younger I used to believe my ideal life style was to live way back in a cabin somewhere - isolated and completely cut off from society...

Not anymore. I realize now that people are everything. The woods are beautiful and I'm in love with every tree and animal and bit of moss, but they just can't love me back.

One consolation I have is God. We speak out loud to each other. He's my buddy. There is no one else. Once I tripped going down this steep descent. I was zooming down this eroded creek bed, trying to make the shelter by nightfall and tripped, falling flat on my face, ramming my jaw into a rock.

"You could die out here STUPID and no one would ever know it," I said to myself. I hike like a maniac, trying to make a shelter by nightfall, in hopes of having the company of other hikers.

The rest of the evening I walked with my arm extended, clutching my hand tightly as though someone was grasping it and saying inbetween sobs, "Jesus, take my hand and walk with me,

be with me."

I wake up in the morning and ask God how things are going so far in His day; if we earthlings are relatively good or bad today.

All day long we talk out loud. If we get lost I say "OK God, we'll stick together and get ourselves out of this; and when we find the trail, we'll sit ourselves down and take a good break."

Does all this sound dramatic and extreme? It isn't. You would never believe you could behave this way, before you left on this hike. You learn FAST how badly you need when you're alone... that it's universal and there is nothing at all wrong with admitting to your weaknesses. In fact, I find this newly acquired humbleness, can actually make you strong.

Coming down off the ridge today, the only vegetation is pine trees and mountain laurel. And all of the mountain laurel is in full bloom. They form big arched columns of beautiful white flowers for you to walk through. And this grand aisle is completely covered with soft pine needles. A bride in the most glorious of cathedrals could not feel more lovely.

I think of my sister back at home... my only sister who is to marry in a few months and I am to be her maid of honor. She writes these heartbreaking letters on how she wants me in her life, to share these important days with her.

The entire family writes me letters like this. And the phone calls are even worse. Sometimes, its very, very hard to be strong.

You have to know what you're being strong for... there must be a reason behind the suffering. I'm not sure I am supposed to be out here anymore. There is a definite gap in my life — an emptiness that has to be filled before I can carry on with the rest of my hike.

Something happened to me yesterday. I'm hurting. I got up at dawn to do my 18⁺ miles a day and I couldn't walk. I am crippled. Everytime I take a step a biting pain goes up my leg. I have to drag my foot to get anywhere. I walked about one mile and sat down and cried. Took off my boot to examine it and it was all red and swollen. What could I have done? I don't remember doing anything in particular to hurt it. A half mile more I try to walk... looking at the trail through my tears and trying to figure out if I should go home or not.

I am getting tired of the trail. I'm doing long days with no spare time to stop and enjoy. There's a kind of compulsion that overcomes me whenever I hike alone. I feel like a machine, cranking in the miles, not really living the trail.

Every view looks the same. Every rhododendron flower smells the same. Every piece of trail just turns the corner and there is another piece of trail. I want to paint. I want to be with my family. I just don't want to be alone anymore.

The verdict at the Waynesboro hospital was a stress fracture. Doc said he could either cast it and send me home on crutches or wrap it and send me back on the trail. I chose the latter. Three days I hike ever so slowly and carefully until I ram it one more time, good and hard. I am broken.

I think that at least half of my injury was brought on by my self, by my own subconscious will to end my heart's suffering. My mind isn't in the woods. I'm not aware of my surroundings, so I'm certainly not going to be aware of the rocks at my feet.

Ramming and ramming my foot into those rocks... I am too tired physically and psychologically to care about picking my feet up.

I am empty and broken and my whole being needs the nourishment of love and human companionship.

It is time to go home and heal.

3 Healed

... early August
after a two-week recovery in Pennsylvania

I had to earn my ticket back into the wilderness.
My bus to Virginia had a lay-over in Washington, D.C., so I
thought that my pack, my stick and I would take in
some sights.

At a red light, a European tourist began asking me
questions, then kissed my hand, then embraced me,
and french kissed me... I thought I had better stop him
before he got carried away even further.

Two down town derelicts chased me up Pennsylvania Ave. because
I wouldn't let them "see" my hiking stick.

The women's lavatory attendant in the bus station screamed,
"Sir, Sir you can't go in there," in front of the entire terminal.
My muscular, unshaven legs were the only thing that stuck out
from my pack.

The bus missed its connection because of a storm, making
it impossible for me to get to the woods by nightfall. At 11:00 I mosey
into the bus terminal, just as they're locking the doors. The local
taxi driver tried to "save" the day by saying "I'll take you
anywhere you'd like to go sweetie. There's room at my place."
... Get me to the woods!

The Pedlar district of the George Washington National Forest is said to be extremely rough. It is. I am fagged going up this first mountain outside of Snowden, Virginia. But I notice I am quite more relaxed this time... just taking my time and not going as far as I can, but as far as I want.

At Fullers Rock I watch the clouds roll in. Rain is coming. Down below winds the James River where I struggled so hard just a few weeks prior.

It's all behind now. Turning and leaving I feel confident in my newly healed body, and my self. I must take care or I'll never get to Maine.

You can't really understand how extraordinary Virginia's Tye River Valley is until you've walked it... until you've traveled down into the valley and climbed back out of it... until the misery is over and you sit back and relish and thank God that it's over.

The 3000' descent and the 3,000' ascent in one afternoon's stroll is not what is so painfully difficult. The misery lies in the obstacle course planted along the way.

There seems to be a problem of maintenance of this section. It can't be trimmed enough. Stinging nettles grow like cancer, reaching way over your head. You must actually swim through them... move them aside one armful after another, before you can take another step. Small pointed rocks lurk in the shadows with their "feet" extended waiting to trip you.

When the plants oil touches your body, you feel like you've been attached by poison darts. This is the epitome of self-control tests, for the more you touch your skin, the deeper you rub the oil into your pores, and the more agonizing it is.

So you walk - SCREAMING! as more and more poison darts bombard your near naked body... all in the intense heat with a thriving mosquito population!

43

Let me introduce the Shenandoah National Park... a 100-mile playground to the thru-hiker... beautifully manicured trails, where in some places the lawn is even mowed. No ascents are steep or badly eroded. Every step is nicely graded... animals walk up to you... deer eat out of your hands... showers every few days at the campgrounds... ice cream sometimes twice a day at the Skyline Drive's frequent stores ... TOUGH LIFE!

There's a 1.8 mile loop trail of the AT in the park and its caption reads, "Hike this section of the famous trail and feel what it's like to walk from Georgia to Maine"... don't kid yourselves, folks!

Tourists annoy some thru-hikers... motoring up to a view in their RV's after we spend half the day climbing, or sprawling over every rock at every look-out.

Much can be gained from these people, though. They love to talk to us, and they'll share everything they have with us.

They live through us, hike through us. Our adventures are the closest thing most will ever get to being a 2,000-mile thru-hiker.

But because people love to frequent this park, it is grossly overused, making the park service inflict a very strict and rigid code of regulations on the hikers. Most thru-hikers become infuriated with this. This is _their_ trail, and they don't want to be told what to do, and as a result, this beautiful park can become a very sharp thorn in some thru-hikers' sides.

Much depends on your attitude. We must learn how to solve the problems of over-population on the trail... the problems of vandalism and ignorant abuse. These rules are the way the Shenandoah Park Service people find best to cope. As hikers walking through, so must we... not only cope, but cooperate and obey, or offer constructive criticism.

One creature I have no desire to share with is a park bear. "Hang those packs high," the ranger said, "Not just the food, but the entire pack. Not alongside a tree but out on a limb."

I just picked up a new food drop. My pack weighs 50 pounds! I can't hoist it up a tree. I can barely get it on my back, so I just hang the food and leave everything else under my tarp, along side of me.

Just about dark I hear this scratching, clawing sound over by the tree. Two beady eyes are watching my every move. For half an hour I keep my flashlight planted on him. I want to know where he is at all times. He slides down the tree, crawls his way back up, swats my bag time and time again.

Flashing lights appear in the sky! The rangers are coming to rescue me! (It turns out to be a terrible thunder and lightning storm forcing me under the tarp and into my bag.)

Don't ask why I don't make noise to scare him. I am alone. I don't want to upset or disturb him. Hell, I can't even think. All I can do is shake and pray.

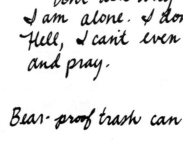

Bear-proof trash can

I shove my fingers into my ears, crawl to the bottom of my bag and try to shut out the world. Half an hour later I wake up to dripping wet nylon covering my body. It's pouring and my tarp has fallen completely down.

For the greater part of the night, I sit with my arm extended, serving as a pole... body cramped up, exhausted from no sleep. When the rain finally subsides, I once more try sleeping. The bear should be gone. Who in their right mind would be out in this weather? Wild animals are! A limb comes crashing to the ground! He got my food bag! Good. Take it and leave please.

Instead, he pads over to a log 15 feet from my head and proceeds to "pig-out" on my week's rations. When he has his fill, he decides to check out what is under the tarp! All through my pots and pans he's going – 6" from my body. The body is quivering. The whistle is poised in the mouth. One paw on me and his going to hear it. The rest of the night he walks circles around me, breaking twigs from time to time to let me know he's there.

When the first shreds of light appear, I sit up and try to inspect the damage. Toilet paper is draped on the bushes. Zip-locks are strewn all over the forest floor. He leaves the gravy mixes, the nutritional yeast and the basil... choosey bear. Tomorrow night I'm going to be with other humans!

Ice cream pacifies me. Good food in general does. When I left my camera in a truck back in the Smokies, I sat by the road crying and consumed an entire package of fig newtons while my partner read excerpts from the Gideons' Bible entitled "In times of extreme sorrow and despair."

Heavenly Hash ice cream is doing the job now... making me forget all about that bear. At least until some tourists approach me with "How's the trail treating you these days?"

Out pours the story. Little tears begin to fall. Then come the sobs. "Come on," they say "You're camping with us tonight. You're not going to be alone." It is Marie and Laton Holton from Norfolk, Virginia. Tonight I am part of their family.

They lay out the homemade quilts and fabulous spread of fruit, vegetables, cheese, soup, stew, and homemade banana nut bread.

But before it all, they thank God out loud for sending me to them... for enriching their lives. They don't know how much their presence means to me.

I am doing my laundry at the Loft Mtn. laundramat when this hiker comes breezing in the door..."You're Cindy! You're the girl who hurt her foot! I've been trailing you for miles!"

I put a request for thru-hikers in a register and Marco Pershell literally ran to catch up to me. Hurray! I am going to have company for the Shenandoahs! Thru-hikers are few and far between these days. It's getting late in the season. Anybody who will make it to Maine this year, is already up north... certainly not down here in Virginia.

All through these mountains we carouse together... driving the tourists and the week-enders crazy.

Marco loves to tell stories and shock the people. He carries toys... frisbee, rubber duck, bones strapped to his pack, a silk tie to wear with his "dress" tee shirt when he goes "out" and his "town hat."

49

Bart and Bill fit right into our "park antics."
These two middle-aged week-enders sport high, influential, respectable jobs but have the happy-go-lucky attitude of 12 year olds.

Bart keeps inviting us to take a few days off at his "cabin." Say no more to a thru-hiker. One offer is all that's necessary.

His "cabin" turns out to be a sauna by a beautiful pond, resting on the side of the Massanutten Mountain range. And his "cottage" is a beautiful swiss chalet nestled in his 300 acres of mountain beauty. We thought we died and went to heaven.

Three days we spent here... eating like kings, swimming, rowing, inner-tubing ... such generous unselfish men. It's hard to believe that people can be this giving when they barely even know us. Who can doubt the goodness of humanity?

I believe in being healthy. If I'm going to drag my body over all these mountains, the least I can do is nourish it properly.

Some hikers' diets are horrifying. One man eats instant oatmeal for breakfast, cheese and prunes for lunch (to counteract each other) and "mac and cheese" for supper, for hundreds of miles, for months on end.

I went the other extreme. I built a dehydrator and for one full year, dried all the food that my partner and I would need for a satisfying and filling 5-month journey.

We made corn chips, wafers, cookies and fudge... all natural ingredients. Every fruit and vegetable imaginable was dried. Herbs for tea and seasoning. Even such delectables as marinated pheasant and dried venison.

Is it any wonder that I never lost one single pound? And is it any wonder that the men love to travel with me, making mealtime into a fantasy come true? "Give me your freeze-dried supper, guys, and I'll combine it with mine and make us a feast."

51

I'm always looking for new ways to spruce up a meal. So enters ... "THE WILD EDIBLE" in flashing neon lights.

High tension power lines are the best source for the succulent greens. We find pokeweed, milkweed, prickly lettuce, dandelion, plantain, and on and on. Every night we incorporate them into our meal... Sauté them in a little butter and garlic powder, or toss them into countless soups and stews.

But the real prize, the real jewels, the real pot of gold that we search for is a BERRY PATCH! Such luscious little gems covering the earth. Hiking schedules completely fall apart when we stumble upon a huge field of ripe, red strawberries.

By mid-summer a thru-hiker can walk, watch blazes, watch rocks, and have his sonar radar out full force; ready to zero in on passing berries. If he's in a hurry, and has to "make tracks," he can pick them WHILE he's zooming by. This is an art... a talent, that is acquired after much diligent practice.

There arent many hikers left on the trail these days... Andy and Doug are two of the few left. We're the late ones, and we've pretty much accepted the fact that we aren't going to make it to Maine... so we relish these last golden days.

Early in my hike, when the shelter was crowded and we slept compacted like sardines, we always made sure when it was time to roll over, we did so on our own pads, without touching another's body.

Now, with my friends so close, if I need to stretch out a limb and someone is there, the leg goes on top or the arm goes around... I love them. What is the big deal about touching or caring or crying or any emotion? This is the beauty of the Appalachian Trail. You can live how you feel. You can be 100% real.

Lying here at night, I roll over to Andy's side and in my half-sleep I smell Andy. I feel secure. The smell is familiar. He is my friend. I roll over to the other side and smell Doug. That too makes me feel good.

53

I'm not talking about "body odor" per se.
That's only when today's moderns neglect to
douse the anti-perspirant and their blocked-
up pores are allowed to flow for a change.
The smell I'm talking about is pleasant.
It's a person's body chemistry and each one
is unique and very individual. After
awhile a person's sleeping bag begins to
smell like them, and their bandana, and
the straps to their pack. I think it's beautiful,
and it brings pleasure to my senses and
comfort to my heart.

There are many misconceptions about
women on the trail. Their ratio to men is very unbalanced and some
think we women have a regular field day.

The Appalachian Trail is not synonymous with a meat
market. We don't travel the hills with nothing but lusty sex on our
minds. The desire crops up, but its far less frequent than in
"normal" life. Everything is put in its proper perspective.
First, we try to survive. Ofttimes that takes all of our energy and
concentration. Secondly, when we meet those of the opposite sex,
we look on them as fellow human beings, not as sex partners.
One very big thing is missing in this type of society. No one is inflicting
any standards, rules of behavior, or perverted conditioning on us, so
we're free to be ourselves. If this trail teaches us anything, its how
wonderfully rewarding relationships can be.

We talk much these last nights about problems of the trail... relocations, road walks, blow-downs, shortage of blazes. Some hikers get all set to storm into Harper's Ferry at the trail headquarters and give them a piece of their mind. That mortifies me. This is our trail now, our baby, and after living it like we are, it becomes our responsibility to see that it goes on living.

Most thru-hikers are not Appalachian Trail Conference members. Most have no concept who these people are or what they're doing for the trail.

Jean Cashin, the Conference's public relations person melted my heart when I walked into the headquarters. She just overflowed with love and concern. It was plain to see that these are a dedicated, hard-working group of people fused together by the love of the trail.

I know where my energies are going to be channeled in the years to come. These people are working to preserve and secure the trail. We must maintain it.

Weaverton Cliffs, just outside Harpers Ferry, West Virginia, is the site of our farewell-celebration. We'll be hiking a few more days, but Harpers Ferry is where we'll leave our hearts.

This is a wonderful time in my hike. A good, whole, complete feeling fills me. We aren't on Katahdin, but we _have_ tried, and we _have_ done our best... we've succeeded in our eyes and that's all that matters.

Our spirits are quiet and our hearts are at peace. Each one of us knows we will finish someday — in our own time, in our own way. For me, it will be in the coming spring.

56

4 Returning

... the following Spring, in May

JoAnn Welsh, my new hiking partner, has bird legs. There is no meat on her anywhere. Her huge pack completely overwhelms her. Her poor knobby knees can't take Pennsylvania's rocks, so she walks with a limp and a crutch and a tear. She has a relapse of tonsillitis. Her system is allergic to bug bites... they swell up to the size of half-dollars all over her body. Every night I set up the tarp, collect the firewood, cook dinner, while she collapses on her bag praying to God for strength. She is a complete greenie, but oh, her determination — and oh, my patience!

I realize what this half of the trip will be for me. My life and my world came together those first 1,000 miles, and my self. Now it's time for refinement. Patience, compassion, understanding will be my constant tools for self-improvement.

#1 Most asked question on the trail...
"AREN'T YOU AFRAID?"

We walked across the Cumberland Valley today. The trail goes from one ridge to the next, all road-walking... over 20 miles. Feet pound on the hard asphalt highway. There's no soft ground to absorb the shock; pounding pain shoots right back into our legs. Heat waves rise from the baking highway flushing our bodies. We exist for the small breezes that oncoming vehicles give us as they zoom by.

All this and my new boots are too small. They were bought before I started in Georgia and the first 1,000 miles has widened my feet considerably. I hurt. I'm walking barefoot across this valley.

I had heard of Joan Ziegler, the postmistress for Allen, Pennsylvania, long before I hobbled into her quaint town.

She brought us home tonight... married only 2 days, still opening her wedding gifts, she invites us to sit on her living room floor and share in her joy. She bought me sneakers and will mail my boots home.

When she left for work the next morning, she replied, "There are eggs and bacon in the fridge." "Help yourself," she yells, as she leaves us alone in the house. JoAnn stares in disbelief, "She doesn't even know us!"

Afraid? Who can be, once you realize how many good people there are in the world to help and take care of you?

It's not 100 feet across to where the ridge steeply drops off to the valley floor. Down below is the rich Pennsylvania farm-lands. The Indians called this ridge "Kittatinny" meaning "endless mountain". It won't stop now. All the way to New Jersey it will go, straight as an arrow, rarely changing in elevation, except for an occasional gap.

We're sleeping on its back bone tonight. I lay with my feet pointing north... toward Maine; my head south, toward the memories of yesterday. My spine against the mountains spine. My entire body has complete contact with the earth.
Right out of the ground the mountain's energy is rising... up, up, filling my entire being.

Rock hopping. That's how we spend our days on these Pennsylvania ridges. There's quite a variety of foot-paths to keep the hiking interesting: from rock hopping huge sandstone boulders on the mountain's crest; to stumbling along loose rock pathways that twist our ankles and make us feel like blundering klutzes; to small, deadly, pointed quartzite rocks firmly secured in the ground, acting as razors, ripping our feet until they feel like raw hamburger. Our necks are board stiff from forever looking down.

Actually, it's not all this bad. There are some nice old woods roads to hike on in Pennsylvania. Some.

And besides, these rock paths lead us to some of the most gorgeous and frequent look-outs on the entire Appalachian Trail; where we can spend countless hours watching hawks and turkey vultures soar and perform spectacular aerobatics.

#2 most asked question
    on the trail...
        "See Any Snakes?"

    Most fears in life stem
from the unknown... snakes
are one of those. We never know where they'll be, how many are in
the shadows watching us, when one will turn up on a rock that
you're using as a hand-hold... so to control anxiety, the best solution
is education.

    First we learn that snakes are not out to get us. They're just trying
to exist in their environment which we are disturbing, so the key
factor here is respect. We learn where they'll be in what temperature,
how they'll act if disturbed and what to do when. We are aware
of the closest road crossing for help. There are so many contra-
dictory theories existing on snake-bite treatment that we just
choose to "get out and get help."

    When in snake country, JoAnn and I make all kinds of racket
to let them know we're coming. We hoot and holler like hunters
driving deer... JoAnn is soprano, I am alto, and since we invented
this preventive method, we haven't seen one snake...
they all run for cover when they hear us coming!

Most people don't know rain. They hide from it in their homes, run from it to their cars. It's a negative thing for them, but it's a way of life out here, for it's rained nearly every day in the past month. Those same people ask, "What do you do when it rains?"... KEEP WALKING.

Keep walking when it's misting, when it's dropping, and sometimes when it blows in gale forces and comes down as sleet and hail and strikes the earth in bolts of thunder and lightning.

My snaps never jived on my homemade poncho from Day 1 on Springer

Mt., so I struggle with rusty safety pins and pieces of string every time the sky falls. The seams around my neck long lost their sealant so I have this constant drip down the nape of my neck... Chinese torture. I place my braided hair there, then the tails of my bandana, then my shirt finally gets soaked.

Soon the rain creeps into every corner
of my body. It runs in streams down
my poncho, onto my legs, saturates
my socks and collects in my boots.
And collects. And collects, until
I'm walking on sponges and water
squirts out of the pores of the leather;
and I must stop every 15 minutes
to wring my socks out, getting nearly
a half cup of water every time.

My nose runs constantly. My
hair is plastered to my face.
There is dirt everywhere on me.
Little pieces of leaves and bark
stick to my wet skin like magnets.

I'm cold. I'm wet. I'm numb. And
hungry because I can't stop to eat
or rest or I'll freeze and all I can
think of is <u>home</u>!

But something must be said for the joys of rain. On those unearthly mornings when I awake and the land is swimming in a warm, misty, opaque fog. Moisture hangs onto everything; every leaf, every branch, every dust particle in the atmosphere. It holds it there until it can't hold anymore and lets go drop by drop, clinging to my eyelashes, thickening my hair, moistening my skin and I'm glad I'm alive and moving through it.

If the temperature is high enough, I needn't wear my poncho... this incredibly refreshing mist bathes and lubricates your body giving me new-found energy.

Frogs and toads seem to jump out and greet me. Brilliant red efts waddle across the trail. Spider webs suddenly appear, holding the moisture and showing off their intricate, fragile framework.

The bark of the trees is considerably darker, almost black, soaked and shining from the rain. The greens of the leaves stand out light and delicate against this strong contrast. The entire forest glistens as if varnished with a heavenly transparent glaze.

You can't know the woods if you only go out in blue skies and shining sun - to love her, you must know her, and RAIN is a face she often wears.

JoAnn is getting stronger. She's finally starting to feel good; so naturally, she's talking of splitting up. She wants to "see" what its like to hike alone. She wants to "see" if she can do it.

We bicker sometimes. Parts of our personalities differ; we're still growing and we have a lot of things to work out with ourselves, but little can be gained from separating.

It's too easy to leave each other every time it goes sour. We will never learn how to give or communicate or co-exist with one another. This trail is our training ground for all our future relationships.

We have a commitment to each other. We're hiking the trail together and we'll make it up Katahdin together.

Sunrise Mt. Pavilion is as romantic a place as it sounds. High on a mountaintop it sits, with a clear view to the east and west. Tonight the entire sky is glowing with a warm pink light and everything is bathed in it... the sky, the trees, the pavilion and us.

This morning we awake to the most heavenly music. Sitting up in our bags, we gaze around us. A blanket of clouds is thrown over the sleeping valley in the early morning chill. The hills poke their heads up like great swimming whales and we wonder if we died and went to heaven.

But there, over on a rock, sits a man playing the most beautiful music on a recorder... for the new dawn, a sleepy-eyed centipede and two blessed backpackers.

We have hailed a bus into New York City at a road crossing. And now, two hours later, we're on Long Island visiting JoAnn's friend Randy, a wonderful Michelangelo drawing show at the Pierpont-Morgan Library and the Ocean.

My life is moving ahead at such a fast pace. Every day I am at a completely different place with completely different surroundings, and with every new area comes new moods and feelings changing in and out, back and forth like a colorful kaleidoscope.

I spend my hours walking on the beach these days... watching sea gulls take off and soar instead of my friends the vultures. Sand is between my toes instead of rag socks. The sea wind is whipping my hair instead of the ridge top breezes, and once again I feel free.

A cold front moved in last night making it 38° where we slept on the mountaintop. Brilliant blue skies greet us this morning and the most exhilarating wind I have _ever_ felt. The "day after" always makes the rain worthwhile.

We're walking through Harriman State Park... it's unbelievable. The forest is predominantly beech and hemlock; the forest floor is very wide open and covered with either hemlock needles or light green flowing grass! _Grass_! everywhere in the forest.

I didn't expect to find such beauty in New York. The trail passes within 40 miles of the city and I thought somehow we'd feel the badness. The only evidence to show that New York is so close is the view at our shelter tonight. We're lying here in our bags, sipping tea and watching the sun set on the Hudson River... and yes, way out on the horizon, way out in the distance is the Manhattan Skyline, with the World Trade Center leading the band!

"All we ask is that you do not be late for dinner"... at the Graymoor Monastery where giving is the byword.

It rests up on a hill overlooking the Hudson, a halfway house for wayward souls (all souls for that matter and hikers must certainly qualify). We're given lodging for the night in our own private suite; fresh towels, sheets, bath, washer/dryer, detergent, water softener, anti-static cling — all for zero money.

Surely we aren't going to be late for dinner. JoAnn and I mosey into the dining hall 25 minutes early — not a soul in sight. We sit down at a huge round table and try to guess what all the place settings are for.

We look at the wine glass and say "It couldn't be." Suddenly a monk, clad in a long brown robe tied with a rope, wearing sandals, comes pushing a cart of red wine. This is only the beginning.

Lasagna, homemade bread, salad, 3 kinds of ice cream with chocolate sauce... all you can eat! Food is available all night long to snack on. We feel like thieves, slipping down at 1 A.M. to fill our bellies. Breakfast is an occasion in itself — eggs, bacon, pancakes, homemade banana nut bread, freshly stewed apricots, prunes and rhubarb.

But this morning, before breakfast, the most incredible thing happens... the real gift of the Graymoor Monastery. It feels like years since my soul had the pleasure of attending Mass, so I'm seeking out the small room where the celebration will take place.

I am the only woman here, or lay person for that matter. Half a dozen Friars sit around in a circle, very intimate, and personal. After the Gospel is read, one Friar, a short balding man, begins sharing his thoughts on the reading... it is about following God's will and being humble and helping each other.

I bring in my feelings of the trail and John and how hard it is for us sometimes. They all seem quite touched that I'm speaking out. At the "Prayer of the Faithful" the balding Friar prays for all the hikers and their sister (myself), for me to find my way. My heart is melting.

At the "Sign of Peace" they all embrace me very warmly and look right into my eyes and my heart and wish me peace.

At the "Breaking of the Bread" the priest uses a loaf of crusty bread and we each break a piece off and pass it to one another saying "Body of Christ"; with the wine saying "Blood of Christ."

The recessional song is "Be Not Afraid" (I go before you always, come follow me and I will give you rest) and I know it must have been picked for me. And let me tell you, I am crying. First my eyes get watery, then the tears come rolling down my face while the Friars all look on smiling.

After Mass my friend comes over, puts his hand on my shoulder and begins asking all about myself and the trail. He insists I have another breakfast and all of us sit around talking mountains and trails. They think it's just wonderful that I came to Mass, but I told them that the pleasure was all mine.

It happened again in Pawling, New York. There's a pavilion at Edward Murrow Park where hikers can shower, swim, and usually rest and relax. Tonight, however, the pavilion is going to be over-run by high school seniors "partying it up"... for their graduation night.

So Mary Kay, the proprietor, invites us into her home. She cooks us a dinner of charcoal steaks, baked potatoes, salad, cauliflower with cheese and fresh strawberry pie... holding hands before dinner we pray together and are grateful.

She sings to us with her guitar and tells us how she had been into drugs and alcohol until she came "home."

I feel at home out here. For such a carefree, uncertain life-style as we lead on the trail, I feel so very secure. When you meet people like Mary Kay, you realize you are not alone in the world; we are all connected to one another and there is such a thing as universal love.

Mt. Alto... it doesn't sound like an evil mountain. It isn't very high, more like a hill, and it's dropping us into Kent, Connecticut, home of another hostel.

We cursed that mountain at day's end. Our bodies are actually steaming as we ascend, so high is the humidity and our body temperature... even our breath is visible.

Darkness is setting in when we finally reach the First Congregational Church, but we make out the sign posted on the door... "These facilities are no longer available to hikers."

We look at each other aghast "It's dark out, there is no choice."

Quietly we creep in, lower our packs, roll out our bags and proceed to wash in the back room's kitchen sink.

JoAnn is on guard duty when she first hears the voices. Here I am, completely nude, sitting in a puddle on the counter, swabbing myself with an old bandana when she yells in a whisper "Oh my God! someone's coming!" Panic strikes! I throw the dirty clothes on my dripping wet body, quickly mop up the sink and she adds, "Never mind, it's just the TV next door."

Sleep came quickly this night, and so does consciousness the next morning when a set of shoes walks across the hard wood floor. "Now what?" The church sexton turns out to be very nice; says there had been some problems but he himself likes hikers just the same and will not say anything.

Quickly, we pack up our homes and go out to face the beginning of a new day and a new state... Connecticut.

The "Cathedral Pines" are awe-inspiring.
I feel the presence of God here like nowhere
before. Walking through them hushed, silent,
and reverent, it feels as though I'm in a
huge, glorious cathedral. I stop. There is
no sound. The trees are so massive,
I almost expect something extremely
powerful to be heard. Just silence, which
in itself is powerful. And all this silence
seems to thunder above everything else
like a huge granite mountain.

Along the Housatonic River there lies a
6-mile stretch of magical, fairy-like pine
forest. The forest floor is so clean and
absent of undergrowth that you half expect
to see little gnome women, under the
towering trees, busy with their sweeping.

Warm orange light floods the forest
floor. Each noble tree wears an orange
stripe painted on its side and all stand
at attention, in perfect rows, honoring
the setting sun.

Certain shelters are known for certain things... bad water, leaky roofs, excellent views. October Mtn. lean-to is famous for its porcupines. When in "porky" country anything with sweaty salt on it must be hung from the shelter's rafters... food, packs, boots, hiking sticks.

About 9 P.M. they start their war hoots. Up in the trees surrounding the shelter they call to one another — back and forth, back and forth like a whining, snorting dog. Then, silence... for near 15 minutes. Suddenly they appear, only a few feet from our heads. Rumps in the air, they begin gorging on the wood.

Flashlights center on the spiny creatures while they do their work. Watch them! I can't lay here letting them consume what so many people took such pains to create. Throwing back my bag, I grab my stick, chasing them right back up the trees. "Git! Git!" I scream, beating every tree I go by.

This is nothing I hear. The porcupines on the Long Trail have such ravenous appetites they even eat fiberglass outhouses

Big mountains lie ahead... Bear Mt., The Taconic Range, Mt. Greylock. Slowly, slowly they grow in elevation and steepness the further north we travel. With each new ascent, our bodies, our stamina, our endurance grows stronger alongside the mountains.

Still, we get very tired. High humidity saps my energy. JoAnn still falls fast asleep upon stopping for a break. "Be strong" my friend Tim writes, giving us encouragement.

We gaze out over the ascending range. We must learn to get over one mountain at a time - confront each day at a time. That is enough. Will be ready for the mountains up north when we get there.

Vermont is definitely a prelude to Maine. Both have exceptional features but because of them, you have the accompanying headaches. Where there are flat sections, there are lakes coupled together causing a never ending mud problem.

Hiking in mud is comparable to walking in quicksand. So much effort is needed to pull our feet out of 4" of dark ooze, and miles of this type of walking is totally exhausting. Thank God for the lakes to wash our caked, black calves and our frustrated dispositions away.

The long Trail of Vermont's crew does a marvelous job of alleviating the mud problem. In many sections, beautifully constructed bog bridges made from split and peeled trees are put in place, both for the hiker's well-being and erosion control.

Today my grandmother is 75 years old. My family is throwing a huge surprise party for her back home.

Today, I also got my period and today we must climb Bromley Mtn.

I DO NOT WANT TO BE HERE!
I DO NOT WANT TO BE IN THE WOODS!
I WANT TO BE HOME!

I saw nothing of the south side of Bromley Mtn. I barely even saw the trail in front of me through my constant flow of tears. The pain in my abdomen... The pain in my heart. Dear JoAnn tries to soothe me by reliving crazy times in high school and college, trying to keep my mind occupied.

As soon as she gets ahead, though, the faucet turns on again. So much to get over... so much to conquer... so much to grow through.

To make our lives worse, we are running out of food ... very, very little remains. Here at Little Rock Pond, JoAnn combines all our remaining suppers into one big dish that will eat cold for the next few days.

But because our dried food lay beside fragrant Safeguard soap for nearly 2 years in the boxes, every dried noodle and dehydrated vegetable reeks with the sickening perfume.

We can't even eat it with our noses held closed. Its gagging.

As JoAnn goes to bury it, I run to the lake. Diving in, I swim and swim out towards the rock until fatigue overcomes me. I lay on my back floating in the cool water and wonder what to do.

— Little Rock Pond

JoAnn is still crying as I go to the caretaker's hut to buy food... tuna, peanut butter and honey, bread, and a huge bag of peanut M+M's... JoAnn's favorite.

They brought little more than a smile as I whip out the goodies atop White Cliffs the next day. Her eyes are red and swollen. Frequently I hear her sniffing and blowing her nose as she hikes.

Our sorrows have gone beyond hunger and mere physical pain. Our hearts are heavy. A definite low point has been reached. We have grown tired of the woods and hiking and look to our next town stop in Killington, Vermont as much needed therapy.

Bed, bath, and breakfast are offered at Mt. Meadow's lodge in Killington, Vt. for a mere $5.00. There's a lake to canoe on, a pool to swim in, and great live music at the Inn at the Long Trail up the road. With all this in mind, our feet are flying down Pico Mtn. leaping over fallen trees. For the first time in a long time, our hearts are light.

Notes were left in all the shelters announcing the big party this week-end and all in all, about a half-dozen hikers come.

We frolic by the poolside in the day... reading, swimming, throwing frisbee. Night finds us boogieing to a great band called DICE - the most versatile, dynamic band I've heard in a long time, with a real hot female sax player.

... what happened our last night here, was just the push we needed to get back on the trail.

Moonlight swimming is next on the agenda this particular evening... our thirst is so strong from perspiring that JoAnn and I both guzzle the cheap wine like it is mountain spring water. 15 minutes later it hit us. I have never been drunk before!

The dear fellow I am with invites me home and being in the condition that I'm in - I accept. By the toilet is where I'm spending my entire evening however... crouched in my wet bathing suit, drooling into the bowl, sobbing... I want to die.

The sickness fades with the early morning light and my brain no longer feels soggy. Slowly, I crawl out to the living room and look around in mortification... "Where am I?" A man descends from the loft. Oh geez, he doesn't even look familiar. "Where did my room-mate find you?" he asks... just let me die!

Returning to the lodge, everyone is seated at the breakfast table with smirks on their faces. Cautiously, I make my way to an empty seat, still feeling woozy. I look down at my food with disgust, for the first time in my life and say to JoAnn, "Thanks pal, for all you knew I could have been lying by the lake - drunk all night." "I knew you weren't," she replies, looking equally as bad, "I was there most of the night."

Five miles we only made today... we are still drunk. Walking into trees, crawling over bridges on our hands and knees - we certainly got what we asked for in Killington - one town stop to remember.

Perhaps we should stick to the woods for awhile; at least to mountain spring water!

5 Getting Strong

Dartmouth, New Hampshire...

    I fantasized about this town long before we arrived. An ivy league college – over-flowing with knowledge, art, music, and young creative energy... lying at the foot of the most glorious mountain range in the east – the White Mountains of New Hampshire.

    Three days have passed here – eating frozen yogurt, egg rolls and gatorade at Thayer Hall; throwing frisbee on the green; visiting art exhibits and transcending in their music library.

    As I sit back, Vivaldi's "Four Seasons" is coming through my head phones, filling my entire being. I close my eyes and feel the peace in my soul and my world. Such divine music – such unearthly music – man striving toward perfection... searching for truth and beauty and trying to become one with God.

In the woods you develop such subtleties, senses become so sharp... Tuning into the far off warble of a bird, hearing creatures scurry into the grass as you pass by, and the wind advancing as it brushes the tops of the trees; feeling the air get thicker and thicker with moisture. At the same time your tissues begin to swell and bloat, putting pressure on your brain and blood vessels; making it harder to flow and harder to breathe and harder to be pleasant... getting to know your body and the world you're moving through.

Then you descend into such an extraordinary place as this... beautiful music, beautiful works of art, what more can an individual ask from life? Being healthy and strong, in good company, plus having all your creative desires fulfilled.

God, what a wonderful, wonderful life!

It takes all afternoon to get up Smarts Mountain. We must hike differently now- slower, steadier, no "blasts" up mountains with 3-5 mile long ascents.

There's a little ritual we perform before climbing. Bodies are stripped at the last creek; clothes soaked in cool water and put on dripping wet. The entire head is submerged; bandanas are soaked for brow wiping and one last quart of water is thrown down the chest.

This is absolutely the only way we can keep our body temperature down and get up these mountains. And 9 times out of 10, we're completely dry upon reaching the summit.

A canned ham bummed a ride up Mt. Mousalikee. Our dear Italian Mothers don't want their little darlings going hungry. Before shipping off a box they fill it with goodies to consume in town. It would take a week to eat all the "town food" though... canned shrimp and crabmeat, a cake, beer pretzels, fig newtons and pineapple juice.

Mom is going to Mass for us today. She thinks it's our last day on earth. I'm beginning to wish it were. We heard horror stories about this mountain and naturally relayed them home. I feel better when I know someone is worrying about me ... shared concern.

Actually, the climb isn't any worse than what we've been used to. slow, steady, and sweaty. Descending is the killer, especially on poor JoAnn's knees. Some sections are so steep, wooden steps had to be drilled and secured into the rock slabs. Other places there are cables and metal hand holds, but mostly only tufts of grass and roots to hold on to.

There's a new man in our lives—
David Josten. A 19-year-old blonde,
German mountain man. He is our
guide over these White Mountains—
our constant companion. On long
grueling ascents, he plays word games;
keeping our minds occupied. He sings
to us, laughs with us, rubs our backs
at day's end. He offers his stick when
climbing and his loving heart when
we are low.

David would like to think we
could not make it without him.
Perhaps we couldn't. At least our
days would not be filled with sunshine if his presence were gone.

A look of tension covers my face. Worry tenses my brow. In a few short minutes we will be above tree line on the Franconia Ridge. Light rain has been falling all day and shows no sign of stopping. JoAnn, David, and I huddle over the stove, amidst the last remaining scrub pines, building our strength and our courage.

Fighting to stay upright is our main concern once on the ridge. Even hiding behind huge rocks, the powerful wind finds us, plastering our ponchos around our bodies like tight skin. I do not want to be overly concerned. JoAnn turns around, yelling through the fog and the wind..."Smile. We're making memories." I just don't want to be foolish. Friends of mine were picked up bodily and thrown yards from where they stood, on these exposed ridges.

Thunder and lightning arise without warning, with the closest tree being miles over the side. This is not a comforting thought.

That quickly, the heavens rumbled. Let's get going! I pull in my sail of a poncho and literally run from the descending black clouds—up and over Mt. Garfield—it seems like miles. Raindrops pelt the tin roof of the shelter as we dive into safety.

Yes, we're making memories!

On the phone in North Conway, New Hampshire - a little town down from Franconia Notch, Mother informs me that somehow, I lost my art scholarship at school. Walking to the laundromat to meet David and JoAnn, my eyes well with tears... We drop into town to do laundry and buy some food. Where we are going to spend the night, we haven't the foggiest; what I am going to do with my future, I haven't the foggiest.

Tom and Winnie Hardy are from Massachusetts, but they vacation in their second home outside North Conway most of the summer months. They overhear us discussing the present dilemmas and invite us home. "Anything you see, that you want - it's yours," Winnie offers of her well-stocked kitchen. A more generous, kind couple you could never meet. They are washing our clothes, feeding us, we are swimming in their indoor pool and talking of life and goals and goodness.

I've always wanted to live on a farm in the mountains and paint... Tom convinced me to go for it. When one dream shatters - begin reaching for the next... I am realizing that my life is definitely unfolding as it should.

"You're going to die," the descending week-enders tell us. "It's so steep and long" they add as we clamber up the Webster Cliff Trail; but they don't know where we have been.

The Webster Cliffs... one joyous adventure. The wind is such an exhilarating temperature since the storm has passed. It seems to blow constantly at this altitude. I open my mouth and gulp it in. The sun is streaming incredible energy into every muscle and pore... getting high on sunshine and mountain breezes. It's actually intoxicating!

The cliffs are extraordinary. Such exposure. Never have I looked straight down a mountain at such an acute angle. Below, the thin ribbon of highway threads through the mountains where we left our friends such a short time ago.

Turning the corner, we are hit by one of the most impressive sights we have ever laid eyes on... Mount Washington and the majestic staircase of the Southern Presidentials.

I gaze long at that mountain. I have dreaded it, desired it, passioned for it. The strongest wind in the world has been recorded up here - 230 MPH. It looks like a king on a mighty throne amongst servants... demanding undue respect.

My feet rock hop across the Presidentials while my head scrapes heaven. I swat black flies and wipe my brow from the sun. The ridge is open - wide open. Eighteen consecutive miles to travel above tree line; but the wind is a mere 15 MPH today compared to the already 200+.

Gentle, gentle southern "Presies" - they are my favorite. The path is smooth. The climbing easy. You can keep your head up and marvel at the beauty that's around you.

Heavy construction is going on at the summit when we arrive.
A new summit house is in the making. Jack hammers rattle; kids
scream. It doesn't bother me. I look through it. To me, this mountain
is sacred. This entire range is sacred. The Cog RR and the auto road
is the only way some folks will ever see this
magnificent world of mountains... I can share.

The Northern Presidentials... huge,
granite sentinels all lined up; rugged
soldiers with rocks and boulders
strewn everywhere. A tight knot
grows in my neck. While I am
so busy looking down watching
my feet, rain clouds begin
enveloping the peaks. Down I
trot into Madison Hut, with
the impending storm lowering
over me.

Tonight we are treating ourselves to a hut visit, ran by the
Appalachian Mtn. Club; truly a
well-earned luxury after traversing the entire Presidential range
in a single day.

94

Our friends from N. Conway, Tom and Winnie Hardy are picking us up at Pinkham Notch today... more rest and relaxation!

While JoAnn and Winnie food shop for dinner, Tom takes David and me for an open-cockpit airplane ride! Dive bombing into mountains, the ride is one continuous scream of joy.

After a shower, a super meal and a nap, some of Tom's friends come over and begin telling us of this "really great band in town featuring an excellent female vocalist who plays a mean SAX." JoAnn and I look at each other "DICE!"... the band we heard at the Inn at the Long Trail in Vermont, 150 miles ago.

We spruce up in our "town cords" and cotton shirts and enter the bar singing "Going Down the Trail Feeling Bad," the song that made us famous in Vermont. "Oh my God" we hear. The singing stops. All is quiet. "I don't believe it," the sax player says into the mike. "Folks we drove here from Vermont. But these folks... these folks WALKED!" We proceeded to be the life of the dance floor ONE MORE TIME!

I wonder if I'll ever be strong enough to take on a mountain without a huff, without a pain, without a struggle. Eighteen-hundred

miles ago I began. Now, my muscles are like rocks; my legs are like trees. My heart is unbelievably strong. Still, Maine's Mahoosic Mountains are trying to destroy us. Increase the humidity. Increase the pack weight. Increase the number of ups and downs and we turn back to wet dish rags.

Mt. Success, our first mountain in the Mahoosic range, is aptly named. We certainly have to earn her summit. Halfway up I collapse. JoAnn follows. Usually she chants "I'm dying. I'm dying," on an ascent. This time its "I'm dead"—PAST TENSE. My sentiments exactly.

Its hard to describe the tremendous fatigue involved in traversing this range. Its not a single pain like a pulled knee or a cracked foot, but a total, complete exhaustion, with sweat pouring out as if all the plugs in your pores were pulled, and that 85% or more water was gushing out.

The sign on the post reads:

MAINE – NEW HAMSHIRE STATE LINE
OLD SPECK FIRETOWER   11.13MI→
GRAFTON NOTCH   12.73MI→
BALDPATE, EAST PEAK   16.65MI→
MT. KATAHDIN   279.00MI→
            MATC

96

There's a deep slash in the Mahoosic Mountains - as if a sword were driven deep into its guts. Huge boulders rolled down its steep slopes creating caves and crevices for us to crawl through. This is the Mahoosic Notch - one of the most famous trail personalities.

Wire directed through the rock shambles by arrows; some of them as big as cars and houses. Ice coats the rocks in the lowest places and crisp, cold air rises from the holes as if someone opened a freezer door.

We choose not to go everywhere the arrows direct us. By careful eyesight evaluation we determine that our bodies are not as small as the holes which we are instructed to cram ourselves into.

On such occasions we detour and it almost has the best of us. JoAnn is clinging to the side of the gorge - stepping on boulders and grabbing for saplings as she goes. One rock is split in two. She steps on the outer half - quickly scrambling for a root to grab, while every muscle in her body seems to turn to JELLO.

I lie with my back against a very wet, mud-eroded rock — my left foot on a tree root, my right one dangling. "Stretch, for God's sake! Grab for the tree!" The strength is leaving me. My limbs begin to tremble. I feel myself slipping." "Get ahold of yourself!"

We meet at the end and try to compose ourselves. The adrenalin surges leave us feeling weak and spongy. Two and a half hours it took to traverse that notch — a distance of one mile!

At this point it isn't clear why the trail can't slab the side of the mountain, instead of driving us right down the middle of the gorge.

Our answer is clear as we ascend up Mahoosic Arm. Straight up over roots and rocks and slippery moss. Later we discover that five injured people were pulled out of this section by helicopters in the past three years!

Screams of delight are rising from the thundering water of Frye Brook as we pull into the adjoining shelter.

There, tumbling over a twenty-foot vertical drop is the infamous Frye Brook Flume. This is no ordinary waterfall. It's a shoot; a slick slide of smooth rock with a thin stream of water lubricating the run. I watch the guys cautiously plot one hand on the far side of the flume and another on the closest. Easing their bodies into it, just at the correct angle... zoom! they take off like a bolt of lightning

I'm not passing up this chance. It's one of those things I'll regret later if I let the opportunity pass me by. With excellent coaches, I am soon going down with very little fear, but with stupendous excitement!

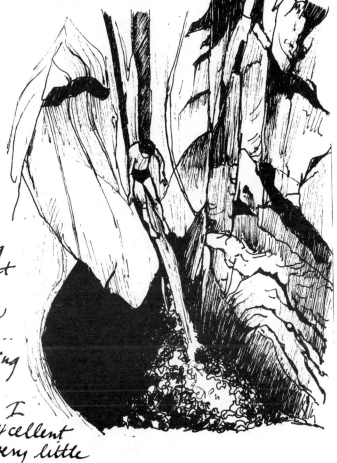

When you share intensely precious times with people... heightened pieces of your life - quality living - a tremendously tight bond is formed between those individuals involved. A fusing of their souls and spirits takes place. It's as if the clouds parted and you had a glimpse of what is really truth and what is really beautiful and what is really lasting in life.

This phenomenon occurred on Saddleback Mountain. It began quite unordinarily. I'm "bringing home" dinner this particular evening... a tender young grouse that I killed with a rock. Everyone staying at the mountaintop cabin is joining in for the mealtime celebration- Don, Beth, Peter, JoAnn and myself; From gutting and cleaning the bird to gathering wood for the roast. We all sit around the warmth, sampling the honey-basted bird, feeling quite wild and independent.

Entertainment is prevalent out here on the trail. And we pay for it, in our own way. The sweat and toil and strain is necessary fare for the vistas at our feet. This evening, on Saddleback, the heavens put on an unbelievable light show for us.

A dramatic storm is moving over Rangley Lake into the valley below. Every 10 minutes the sky changes drastically. Long arms of golden light reach down from the clouds, striking the water... giving the appearance of liquid gold poured on its surface. As the storm approaches, we can actually see rain pouring down, drenching the valley. Shortly afterwards, little pellets of hail send us diving to the safety of the cabin.

This cabin we're staying in is really a broken-down shack adorning the mountain's summit. By the light of day it's a horrid eye sore, with dirt and trash and rusty sardine cans everywhere. But as darkness over takes the day, the softened candle-light transforms the shack's hard edges and it appears almost quaint.

Hail beats on the tin roof, wind bangs the shutters — but we all feel very safe and secure inside.

I almost feel like making the rounds and kissing my new friends good-night, so close do I feel to them. It's like being home. My insides are as warm and glowing as this candle burning by my side.

The Saddle back storm brings in a huge cold front, making clear bright days and unbelievably cold nights. We hike with bandanas on our heads, eat with socks on our hands at dinner; every article of clothing is worn to bed.

Here in Maine the season is changing. Yellow birch leaves line the trail. The Clintonia has blossomed, berries have ripened to a deep blue and dropped off. All you can see around your feet are browning Clintonia leaves. My, have we watched them progress.

I walk the trail now and try to record its life in my head... make it clear and distinct and indelible... those things which make the woods and this way of life home to me.

My daily constant companions are the ferns on either side of me - the hobelbush, the bunchberry, a carpet of moss covering everything. After it rains, I lean down to drink water right off the trail. This state is so impressive and beautiful to me.

Today was one of those impressive Maine days—
those rare, waking moments when you seem to function on
a higher plane of living. Walking the last miles of the
day, I became very emotional. I don't want to see
the day end. I look at the low light
streaming through the forest like it had
never really been seen before.

My hands brush around the bark
of trees and my finger tips long
to linger there.

My entire being is sending
out feelers to the world around
me. Gosh, I don't want to
leave the woods this evening,
but another oasis waits in
Stratton... the Whipple Inn.

The upstairs of the barn has been converted into a meager, yet grand inn for hikers. Very comfortable mattresses with feather pillows, an old fashioned bath tub, towels and a tremendous breakfast are only some of the features of the Whipple Inn.

Janine, the owner, cooks us a fabulous breakfast of whole wheat pancakes with grated zucchini, pure maple syrup, fresh goats milk, eggs from her chickens, and real coffee is brewing on the wood stove.

I woke up to a rooster crowing this morning like I've always dreamed. I hear the goat making familiar goat noises. The Polish pole beans are climbing up their runners and the kids are running around in their underwear in the warm morning sun. The existence seems idyllic. Its the kind of place that makes you want to linger. I long for this lifestyle sometimes, and I get over anxious to get on with the trail and move onto a new piece of my life.

Everyone's feelings are fluctuating these days. After the extraordinary number of mountains we've just been over, we are physically and psychologically worn out. The people like Janine and the places like the Whipple Inn recharge us and encourage us to savor the moments that are left - because before too long, they'll be memories.

105

There's a definite magic in the Maine woods. Never have so many extra ordinary events happened so frequently, and our evening here at Pierce Pond is a prime example.

The trail leading here is extremely muddy, and I'm wearing myself frazzled from pulling my feet out from the mud's suction. Tonight I'm going for a swim, no matter how chilly the evening air. Cold shock surges through my body as

I plunge head first into the mirrored lake. Lying back in the refreshing numbness I think of my friends so close by. Don, Beth, and JoAnn are here. Dear David Josten, our White Mtn. guide is back, and a few others. Little do we know, the heavens have another enchanting show planned for us.

It begins with a very dramatic sunset and one by one, as each star turns on, the loons begin laughing way off on the far side of the lake. Wild, eerie sounds fill the twilight. We sit around the lake feeling very much like the first explorers into the Maine wilderness must have felt.

Then, great bands of light pulsate across the sky- widening and narrowing, setting off rays, getting brighter and dimmer. We are witnessing the wonderous Aurora Borealis!

Lying back on our foam pads, we ooh! and ahh! and clap! Such entertainment! Then- a meteorite shower comes on the heavenly screen... little, darting glimmers of light shooting through the sky. Yes, the pain and discomfort are worth it on such rare and fascinating nights as these.

On this side of Pierce Pond lies the "Carrying Place" - a hunting lodge offering a delicious breakfast of "all you can eat" pancakes. Some men manage to slide 18-19 pancakes - the men who will be fording the Kennebec River, only a few, fast-moving miles away. It's the most famous ford on the entire AT. In some parts, the water climbs to your hips. It's swift and treacherous with smooth, round rocks covering the river's floor, forcing hikers to keep their boots and socks on while traversing.

Beth Ellen and I are carrying very expensive camera equipment -

our pride and our egos are not large enough to face that river - not when there is dear Howard Smith waiting to ferry us across in his rowboat for a mere $10.00 a head.

The "town" of Caratunk lies on the far side of the river. The gas station, post office and general store are all located under one roof. Here, the question arises amongst all hikers, "How did you get across?" We all chime in... "We took the boat and we're proud!

108

We're sleeping atop Moxie Bald's Firetower tonight. The women that is. A candle flickers in the window and giggles rise in the night, as we talk about childhood and old sweethearts.

The men lie down below- looking up at the romantic sight, they call to us, "Rapunzel, Rapunzel, let down your hair."

Five A.M. finds us all together waiting for the sunrise. Huddling together in our bags, eating prunes and witnessing the birth of a new day. Blankets of rose-colored clouds engulf the lake wilderness and here and there little pimples of mountains rise above the cloudy sea.

Seven o'clock and our eyelids grow heavy... naptime... with swimming scheduled at high noon only 1½ miles down the mountain. All days should be like this.

109

Monson, Maine, is a turning point for us. It's the last town stop before entering the last stretch of the AT— a virtually inaccessible 100-mile wilderness. Nearly all mountains come to an end here, and days of swimming and sunning abound.

Tar and dirt roads lead the way into town. We hike side by side in the rain, singing old camp songs, eating wild roadside apples and getting soaked. We don't care. Shaw's Boarding House is at the end of the line.

We immediately like Keith Shaw. He's a short, strong, balding man. He takes to John and I and invites us back the next year for moose season. Pat, his wife is busy canning green tomatoes as we step into her kitchen. She manages to put a great dinner together for our seemingly bottomless pits.

A few members of our family are leaving us— dear Beth included. Some will return at Katahdin Stream Campground to join us in that memorable climb. Our relationship with these new friends is almost sacred. People don't experience such heightened life— go through what we've gone through together and go away unaffected. We've touched souls, and the bond that was created will grow stronger and stronger as years go by. Of this, I'm sure.

6 The Final Days

How do I begin to write about Maine's wild lake country?
A world so wild and pure and sacred. It is my Utopia...
my dreamland. The Smokies were beautiful - Vermont, New
Hampshire incomparable. But Maine. Oh Maine. Never have I
seen such untouched beauty.

Her lakes and balsam firs. The mosses and moose. Frequent
rains and glorious sunlight streaming through pines. The loons.
Morning on misty lakes. The smell of deep forests, bright orange
mushrooms, brilliant yellow lichens.
The wet trail, the roots, beaver dams, the
hammering of wood peckers. Glittering sunsets,
the moonrises star-filled nights and the
majestic northern lights.

We are in the last stretch of
Maine woods: the 100-mile lake wilderness. No roads, no stores, no week-enders,
no civilization - just wilderness.

We are nearing the end of our journey
and its time for reflection.

I think of how I spend _so_ much of my day. My hand wrapped around my stick; my fingers know just where the little knob is on top and they are comfortable. I hold it differently for different types of walking. On ascents, the knob helps push me up those mountains, and eases me down more gently... a real friend, my stick.

I am used to feeling the breeze as I sleep. I am used to sitting and stretching out on rocks and watching the distant mountains and close-by valleys. I am used to feeling the earth beneath my body as I sleep and wake up very early to a new dawn. I am used to drinking clear, fresh water. I desire no other beverage. These things have become ingrained in my being — part and parcel of my soul and I wonder what my life will be like when I must leave all this behind.

Bodfish Farm is our goal for today's hike. Since it's mentioned in the guide book, we figure it will be a normal-day farm. We'll ask to sleep in the barn, get water from the creek.

We descend into this small valley with its ramshackled buildings and trailers... dogs, cats, trash, old cars, furniture everywhere.

Donovan, the owner of Bodfish, comes out of his doorless trailer, shakes our hands, and invites us in for the night. "NO THANKS! We'll choose a patch under an apple tree."

His two young children are 12 and 15 years old and they join us for the evening. The poor things look so wretched... dirt-covered bodies, smelling like urine. With empty stomachs they look on as we eat our dinner. I take them gathering apples to cook down for sauce, in hopes of filling them up.

Donovan is 75. His wife is 40. She lives across the dirt road in another trailer with her boyfriend — neither seem to care about the children.

Again, Donovan invites us into his rat-trap trailer and until it starts raining, we stoutly refuse. He shows JoAnn and me to a "bedroom" with old tools and rusty metal everywhere. Our last thoughts as we force our eyes to sleep... "If our parents could see us now!"

The next day we discuss the place. We feel sorry for the children. They are dying for love and affection. The little girl says her Mother hates her. She clings to JoAnn's hand and never leaves her side. The boy takes to me and follows me around like a shadow, even carries my pack up the mountain behind his "home."

We realize that all homes are not like ours, all parents, all families are not like ours. How well we are blessed!

Tonight we are going to play house. Old Antler's Camp by Lower Jo Mary Lake has furniture, a wood stove, beds with mattresses, linoleum floors. Tomorrow we'll go fresh water clamming and have ourselves a feast. Depression is setting in again. We're on food rations, and get weaker and hungrier each day. It isn't the hunger that has us feeling low, but the fact that we must now go faster through this glorious wilderness, just to make ends meet.

Bunchberries

We've been poking and playing in the lakes longer than we had anticipated, or our supply allowed. We try to fill up on pithy, red bunchberries for extra energy. It's colder now too. Autumn is approaching and it takes more fuel to keep our bodies warm. Jo Ann and I grow closer each day. When we go through hard emotional times and need each other for support, we grow in quantum leaps.

Beautiful warm sunlight streams into the cabin this morning. The lake outside is like a mirror, reflecting the intense light. It's going to be an exquisite day.

We walk around the lake to find the sand beach where there are fresh water clams. The morning sun warms the lake water. We don our boots and walk out to mid-thighs, stretching our arms deep down to pick up the clams. They will be our lunches and our suppers for the next couple of days.

A strange, strange phenomenon occurred today. We stumble down to Nanamakinta Shelter, weak from lack of nourishment, eyes damp and mumbling prayers. There, in the shelter are mass amounts of food that someone miraculously left. Gallon jars of rice, oats, macaroni, instant pudding; even butter and salt for our clams! This never happened before.

May I add to St. Augustine's Five Proofs of the Existence of God... #6 Hike the AT, put your faith in God, and see how well you're taken care of.

For me, there is no other mountain greater than Katahdin. It is the end. The epitome. For nearly 2,000 miles the mountain has been in my head, in day dreams, and night dreams.

When I first saw it, it was like seeing God in the parted heavens, lying so close to Pemaduncook Lake – so very close and distinct. Rising above the evergreens it seems to speak to me... "Come. One last struggle. Up this mountain and it will be all over." My reason for hiking, for struggling, for sweating and paining will be fulfilled on that lofty peak, now only a distant eye ful away.

It was as if the mountain did not exist before. I had never laid eyes on it. I began to think of it as something intangible and untouchable.

But here it is – looming in clear reality. I am totally overwhelmed. I kneel in reverence. It stands for everything I believe in – God, nature's wildness, believing in myself and the realization that dreams really do come true.

117

These last days approaching Mt. Katahdin are the most stimulating. Winding closer and viewing her more intimately with every lake we round... we are preparing for the end.

It is time I ready myself for the return home. This will come as a shock, I'm certain. It seems like years since I have been hiking. Living in the woods has become a natural way of life. Somehow, something must be found to take the place of the extraordinary pleasures received from living and traveling in the out-of-doors. New needs have been made. Freshness and wildness must be ever present in my life.

These needs must be continually satisfied and fulfilled or I know a part of me will die – the most essential part of my being

... my spirit.

On this trip, there has been no greater pleasure for me, than having JoAnn by my side. When two people sweat together, cry together thrill together, something happens. A bonding of hearts and spirits takes place... a fusing of souls.

JoAnn has sunk with me and flown with me. There is little I could hide from her. She knows me like no other. She has been with me where no other has.

Like two young plants we have grown together in the sun. Struggling to keep alive, struggling for room around us to grow— but always together.

This means everything to me. She has shown me that the real beauty of the Appalachian Trail is not just living in harmony with nature, but with each other; our success cannot be measured by merely reaching Katahdin, but by fulfilling this goal, this mutual dream ... together.

Watching the sun set on Dasey Pond and Mt. Katahdin is like sitting in an easy chair before a glowing fire... peaceful and reflective after a hard day's work.

We canoe around the pond, bathed in rose-colored light. Our oars cut through the still water and our voices cut through the evening air. We harmonize and chant Indian songs, offering our music to the mountain God.

Morning is a celebration. The sun rises on the right side of the peak, as gold mist rises from the pond.

JoAnn and I stop on our walk to Katahdin Stream Campground to meet our friends. We stop in time and look into each other's eyes. Let us remember this day of days. Let us not lose sight of what this moment means.

We are all together again - Don, Beth, JoAnn and I.
Being together for this memorable climb will be, we hope,
the cement that keeps us as one spirit for many, many years
to come.

Gradually we ascend until we hit the rock boulders -
"The Gateway" to the world beyond... above tree line. I pull my
body up the iron hand holds planted in the rock. My legs
shake. It happens when I push too hard, too fast. Donaldo
comes up from behind and puts his hand on my shoulder
and in a quiet, understanding way says, " How are you Cindy Lou?"
"Tired... real tired," I answer, as my eyes brim with tears.
"Me too," he adds. We
slept little last night.
It was unseasonably
cold and the excite-
ment of the coming day
was intense.

The impact of the day
is draining me. Such
heights of emotion
flood my being as I
walk across the table-
land - the huge, mile-
long peneplain leading
to the summit.

"You can't hike trails the rest of your life," folks tell me. Well, as much as I love it, I really don't want to. There are other goals in my life that need fulfilling.

Perhaps something must be said for immobility - for being stationary. Roaming... especially being footloose in the wilderness is just plain incredible. I've never felt more alive or free in any other situation.

But I have a strong need to give something back to the world. After it has given me so much. It taught me, made my heart gentle, gave me understanding and wisdom. I feel now I must return some sort of positive addition to mankind.

I hike for no immediate reason. It's the person I <u>become</u> when I hike that drives me to continue. I know I'll return. Isn't the trail what life is all about? The joys, the sorrows, and pains are there, but mostly the love between fellow human beings.

Baxter Peak lies an eternity away, as my life does, dropping off into uncertainty. Small tufts of alpine flowers nestle between rocks at my feet. The sun is warm; the air still. The drama is building, mounting.

JoAnn and I cling to each other, support each other as we have these last thousand miles. We collapse at the summit, embracing the sign and each other... tears pour from our trembling faces... champagne bottles pop... cameras click.

Intense joy fills my being. A deep, powerful scream rises from the depths of my soul... it echoes throughout the Great Basin and the world beyond... it flys through the air like a majestic eagle, who truly knows what freedom is.

Hurray! It is finis!

The "other" world has its problems. We didn't come out here to escape, but to learn how to make it better and acquire hope.

This trail taught us that God is still present in the world and goodness is still present in human beings. Not only present, but beautifully alive. That was proved time and time again.

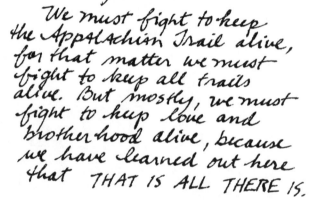

We must fight to keep the Appalachian Trail alive, for that matter we must fight to keep all trails alive. But mostly, we must fight to keep love and brotherhood alive, because we have learned out here that THAT IS ALL THERE IS.

The End

KATAHDIN
BAXTER PEAK
ELEV. - 5267
NORTHERN TERMINUS OF THE
APPALACHIAN TRAIL

NATIONAL   A MOUNTAIN FOOTPATH EXTENDING
SCENIC   OVER 2000 MILES MAINE TO GEORGIA
TRAIL
        1.0 ← THOREAU SPRING
        5.2 ← KATAHDIN STREAM CAMPGROUND
       14.5 ← WEST BRANCH PENOBSCOT- ABOL BRIDGE
      276.0 ← MAINE - NEW HAMPSHIRE STATE LINE
      327.0 ← MT. WASHINGTON, N.H.
     2025.0 ← SPRINGER MT. GEORGIA
PLEASE DO NOT DEFACE SIGN HAPPY HIKING!

Shortly after returning from the trail, I moved to a farm by Hawk Mountain, Pennsylvania... a stone's throw from the Appalachian Trail. Here, I paint and write, maintain a section of the trail, and bring home hikers to help remind me of it. I hike nearly every day - camp out once a week - back pack once a month. You'd think this was enough. (My parents think it's more than enough). It's not. Right now I'm preparing for another long hike... the Pacific Crest Trail. I can't stay away; I'm totally addicted.

I have learned that you *can* hike trails the rest of your life. If that is what brings you the most happiness and peace, then that is what you *must* do.

We also learned that if you don't want life to be a major disappointment when you return, you must have other loves, other things to believe in. Here lies the major problem for most thru-hikers. They look for a passion to rival the trail.

But life is made up of ordinary days. The challenge lies in making some big moments out of those ordinary days. We all can't set the world on fire. We have learned a tremendous lot out there and the world needs to hear it. Simple things, but important lessons, like how to love and hope and trust. We _are_ better human beings because of that long walk and we owe it to the world to be positive assets to mankind - to shine.

I hope this book brings a little glimmer of that light into your world ... by opening up these pages and opening up my heart to you - you may come to believe in a better world as we do.

... for this opportunity, I am so, so grateful
Cindy Ross

To my Appalachian Trail friends...

"I want to say something to all of you who have become
a part of the fabric of my life.
The color and texture which you have brought
into my being have become a song, and I want to sing
it forever.
There is an energy in us which makes things happen
when the paths of other persons touch ours and we have to
be there and let it happen.
When the time of our particular sunset comes, our
thing, our accomplishment won't really matter a great deal.
But the clarity and care with which we have loved
others will speak with vitality of the great gift of life we
have been for each other."

from the album Wherever You Go, copyright 1972, The
Benedictine Foundation of the State of Vermont, Inc.,
Weston, Vt. Composer: Gregory Norbet, O.S.B.